Political Life in
Eighteenth-Century Virginia

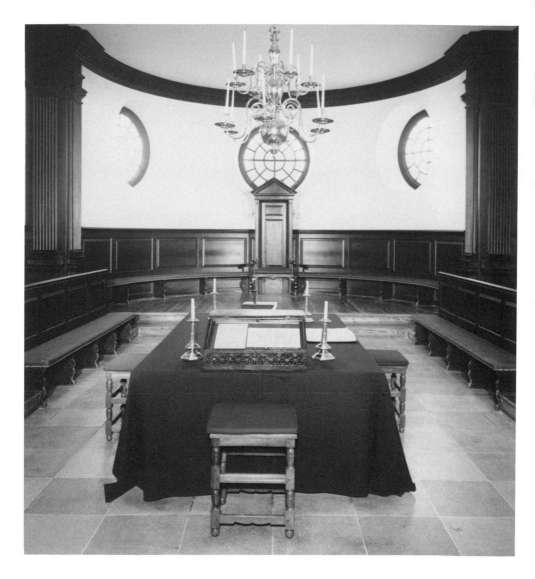

The interior of the Virginia House of Burgesses.

The Foundations of America

Political Life in Eighteenth-Century Virginia

By Jack P. Greene

The Colonial Williamsburg Foundation
Williamsburg, Virginia

Virginia's Political Achievement

During the first three-quarters of the eighteenth century, the free inhabitants of Virginia took enormous pride in its status as Britain's oldest, most extensive, "most populous, . . . most wealthy," and "most prosperous" American colony. During the great events of the American Revolution, it seemed only fitting, as contemporaries from Georgia to New Hampshire acknowledged, that Virginians should take the lead in opposing Great Britain and creating a new American nation. As one French visitor observed in the mid-1790s in repeating a widely shared opinion, Virginia "was one of the first [colonies] to take part in the revolution: and no one of the states made more vigorous efforts, expended greater sums, or displayed more signal energy, to accomplish that happy object."

At every stage of the American Revolution, Virginians played a highly conspicuous role. They seemed, as the Massachusetts lawyer and future president John Adams remarked, to be "at the head of everything." In May 1765, Patrick Henry first sounded the rallying call for resistance with his resolutions against the Stamp Act. In September 1774, Peyton Randolph was elected first president of the First Continental Congress. In May 1775, the Second Continental Congress named George Washington as commander in chief of the new Continental Army. On June 7, 1776, Richard Henry Lee made the motion in Congress for independence from Great Britain, and over the next month Thomas Jefferson composed the Declaration of Independence, next to the Federal Constitution of 1787 the most important state paper produced during the Revolution.

Meanwhile, back in Virginia, in July 1776, George Mason was acting as the principal architect of the Virginia Constitution, the first constitution adopted by any of the thirteen colonies that was declared to be permanent. He also wrote the Virginia Declaration of Rights, the first such document ever to be in-

1

Thomas Jefferson.
Courtesy, Independence National Historical Park Collection.

John Marshall.
Courtesy, Washington and Lee University.

James Madison.

George Mason.
Courtesy, Virginia Museum of Fine Arts.

cluded in a formal constitution of government. Each of these Virginia documents served as a model for other colonies during the rash of constitution-making that accompanied the decision for independence.

During the 1780s, when the American union seemed on the verge of collapse, Virginians again took "a leading, active, and influential part in bringing about" a stronger national government. One of the three authors of the *Federalist Papers* and a prime mover in the drive for a stronger national union in the mid-1780s, James Madison has often been referred to as the father of the U.S. Constitution.

Four Virginians—Washington, Jefferson, Madison, and James Monroe—won eight of the first nine presidential elections held under the new Constitution. The most prominent and influential chief justice of the United States during the early decades of new federal union, John Marshall, yet another Virginian, became the chief judicial interpreter of the Constitution.

Virginia's extraordinary contribution of political talent to the era of the American Revolution has never been equaled by any other state in American history. Indeed, it is perhaps unparalleled in modern history: no single political entity seems to have produced within such a short period so many people who compiled such a remarkable record of achievement in the public world. What kind of a political system produced this astonishing flowering of political leadership? This question has fascinated students of the American past for nearly two centuries. It is the question this book seeks to illuminate.

The Seventeenth-Century Background

Virginia had not always had such a dominant position among Britain's American colonies. To be sure, as the first permanent English colony in the New World, it had always been the Old Dominion, the most ancient of England's American colonies. For nearly a century after its founding, however, Virginia had been a place of doubtful reputation.

Celebrated for the great beauty of its broad rivers and towering forests as well as for its rich soils and its potential as a colony in which free people could make substantial fortunes by producing tobacco for export to the British Isles and Europe, Virginia was still a place that was crude, unsettled, unhealthy, permissive, exploitative, and riddled with violence, conflict, and contention.

With no towns worthy of the name, little organized religious life, and few other attractive cultural features, Virginia society was organized primarily to produce tobacco. The majority of its white inhabitants were young adult males who had been brought to the shores of the Chesapeake Bay to provide the backbreaking labor required by tobacco. Bound by contract to long terms of servitude that usually lasted from five to seven years, they were subjected to such severe discipline and such harsh working conditions that many of them were reduced to despair and bitterly regretted ever having left England.

Tobacco warehouse receipts were commonly used as legal tender in eighteenth-century Virginia.
Courtesy, Cabell Papers, Swem Library, College of William and Mary.

Those who managed to survive often fell victim to disease. Death resulting from malaria, bad water, dysentery, and other diseases was considerably higher than it was in England, where it was by no means low. With a high death rate and a much larger number of men than women, the birth rate in seventeenth-century Virginia was low, and population grew very slowly, largely as a result of immigration. A majority of children grew up as orphans or in broken families, and life expectancy was short. Few people lived beyond the age of fifty.

Not surprisingly in these conditions, political life was fragile. Public leaders were subject to the same high death rate as the rest of the population. For that reason, Virginia did not experience much continuity of political leadership until the closing decades of the seventeenth century. Well into the 1680s, a significant proportion of leaders at the local level and in the provincial government in the capital at Jamestown were immigrants. Some of them were younger sons of respectable English gentry, yeoman, mercantile, or professional families who came to Virginia with some social standing and economic resources.

Many others were self-made men who were able to take advantage of the opportunities they found in Virginia to acquire wealth and reputation. Whatever their origins, however, their attention was firmly fixed upon the main chance. They wanted to establish a stable political and legal system that would secure to them the property they were acquiring in their new home, and they made impressive strides in that direction. But they also tended to look upon public office as a means for their further enrichment.

This mercenary attitude toward public office combined with the low social origins of so many officeholders to make the authority of the colony's leaders highly tenuous. In England, public office was reserved for men of superior wealth, established family, and high social status, and people from the middle and lower ranks of society customarily treated officials with regard. Because so many early Virginia officials lacked all of the traditional English attributes of authority except wealth, however, they did not enjoy similar respect.

On the contrary, a skeptical populace showed little reluctance to challenge their claims and capacity to govern. As one disgruntled inhabitant of York County declared in 1662, it was by no means obvious that a little success in planting tobacco qualified men who had previously been only "Coopers, Hogg trough makers, Pedlars, Cobblers, tailors [or] weavers" to "sit where they doe sit"—in positions of power and responsibility.

As a result, the institutions—colony legislature, parish vestries, and county courts—over which leaders presided and the laws they made and were supposed to enforce also commanded less than universal respect. Like the authority of the leaders themselves, they were always open to question.

Without authoritative leaders, institutions, or laws, Virginia society was loose and had considerable potential for discord. Moral discipline was lax among all social classes. The large laboring population often seemed to be on the verge of social revolt. Yeoman farmers and small planters, men who were not part of the emerging elite, frequently took an active role in politics, and rival coalitions of wealthy tobacco planters vied with one another for the economic spoils they hoped to gain from achieving supremacy in public life.

At the same time, efforts by the English government to secure more control over Virginia's economy and government produced a series of conflicts that threw the colony's public life into a state of strife and discord.

Transformation

Between 1680 and 1730, however, the evidently volatile world of seventeenth-century Virginia was gradually transformed into the much more settled world that characterized Virginia during the Revolutionary era. During those years, black slavery began to displace white indentured servitude as the

This is the only contemporary map of Virginia that shows county lines west to the mountains. It was published in London in 1770.

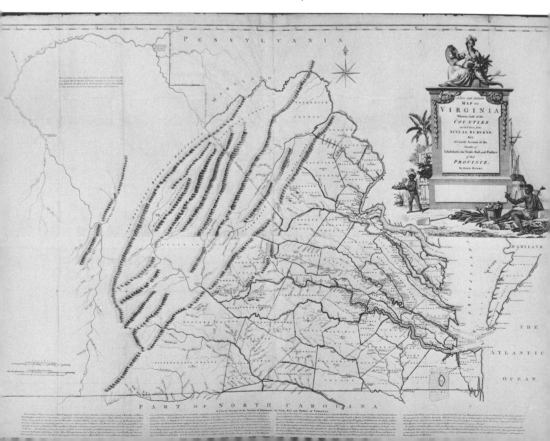

predominant form of labor, and immigration from England slowed down. Simultaneously, improved life expectancy, a more nearly equal proportion of women to men, and earlier marriages raised the birth rate and led to a more traditional form of family structure with parents and children living together in separate households.

Together, these developments contributed to the emergence of a native-born majority among the white population, which, in the 1680s and 1690s, finally began to reproduce itself. By the 1720s and 1730s, it was growing at the same rapid rate that had long characterized the colonies to the north.

As the population grew and spread out from the Tidewater west up the great valleys of the James, York, Rappahannock, and Potomac rivers toward the Blue Ridge Mountains, Virginia society became far more stable. Still very largely devoted to tobacco production and with no important commercial town, it consisted primarily of a series of scattered rural communities mostly composed of independent yeoman farm families, the majority of whom owned medium-sized farms of from two hundred to one thousand acres that they worked with the help of a few white servants or black slaves.

Increasingly during the first forty years of the eighteenth century, however, these neighborhoods were transformed by the emergence of a few large plantations worked almost entirely by slaves. These complex economic and social units, each of which was almost an independent community within itself, quickly became the principal symbol of Virginia society.

The great families who presided over these plantations usually came from a small but increasingly wealthy native elite composed of the most successful among Virginia's new native majority. Almost all members of the earlier immigrant elite had been primarily interested in making fortunes and, if they survived, returning to England as quickly as they had made enough money to do so. Anxious about Virginia's almost wholly unsavory reputation in England, the new native-born elite self-consciously set about trying to "improve" Virginia by making it more recognizably English.

Born between 1645 and 1685 into economically and politically successful families in Virginia, men like Benjamin Harrison, Jr., Richard Lee, Jr., Ralph Wormeley, Jr., John Custis, Jr., Robert "King" Carter, Richard Bland, Sr., Dudley Digges, Peter Beverley, George Mason, Jr., Philip Ludwell, Jr., Robert Beverley, Jr., William Byrd, Jr., John Robinson, and William Fitzhugh,

Jr., threw themselves into that effort with a verve and a sense of public spirit and community responsibility that had been much less evident among their predecessors.

Such men displayed their commitment to the place where they were born in a variety of ways. During the first two decades of the eighteenth century, they joined with prominent new immigrants like William Randolph, William Tayloe, and the Reverend James Blair to establish an elegant new capital city in Williamsburg and to fill it with imposing public buildings, the brick exteriors of which gave those structures an air of permanence. These included not only a capitol and a palace for Virginia's English governor but also the new College of William and Mary to provide their sons with the advanced learning for which earlier generations had had to go to England or Massachusetts Bay.

They also began to build new brick courthouses in each county and brick churches in many parishes. Less successfully, they also sought to stimulate urban development. Actively cultivating a richer public life, they worked to make existing political and religious institutions stronger and more responsive. Robert Beverley, Jr., a member of Virginia's new native-born elite, even wrote a book-length *History of Virginia*, which

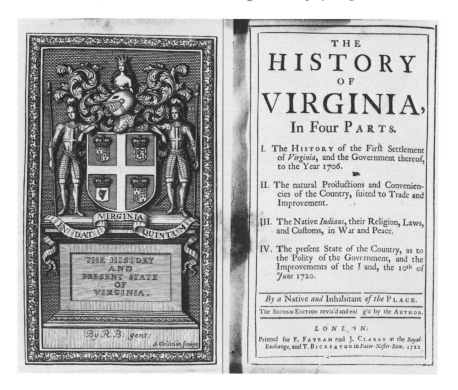

8

Frontispiece and title page of Robert Beverley's History of Virginia.

gave the colony a sense of permanency and legitimacy it had lacked in earlier years.

During the half-century beginning around 1720, the children and grandchildren of this group consolidated their economic, social, and political position within the colony. Along with a much smaller number of immigrants and men descended from less affluent families, they amassed more and more wealth in the form of land and slaves and pursued a gentle lifestyle similar to that of the families of wealthy landed gentlemen in Great Britain.

Referring to themselves as "the gentry," they built grand new brick houses that commanded the countryside and the broad rivers and inlets of the Chesapeake. They entertained liberally and filled their houses with luxury possessions, including imported carpets, silver plate, books, musical instruments, and other items that would help to set them off from the lower ranks of society and to identify them as people of great wealth, status, and gentility.

They provided their sons with the formal classical educations appropriate for gentlemen of English descent. By intermarrying across local political boundaries, they eventually turned themselves into a highly visible and prestigious colonywide elite.

While members of Virginia's native elite thus busied themselves imitating the English gentry and trying to transform

The building of Rosewell, the largest house in colonial America, saddled its owners and their descendants with debts.

Virginia into a more polite and civilized society, they by no means neglected their private material interests. Indeed, throughout the eighteenth century, they not only continued to produce tobacco for an expanding market in Europe, they also eagerly seized upon new opportunities in iron, grain, food, and naval stores production and land development to increase their wealth.

But they gradually learned to control the impulse toward personal accumulation of property that had been so powerfully evident among their predecessors during the seventeenth century. By the 1730s and 1740s, the competitive drive for wealth and power that had been so divisive during Virginia's first century had been largely channeled into much less disruptive pastimes, including horse racing, gambling, and competition for political office. As a result, the gentry became more cohesive and public life considerably less subject to conflict.

At the same time, Virginia's numerous yeomanry became more passive politically. Between 1675 and 1725, these smaller farmers, including even some men without substantial property, had taken an active part in politics, playing a highly visible role in elections and sometimes even finding their way into the House of Burgesses, Virginia's equivalent to the British House of Commons and the oldest lawmaking body in colonial British America.

Over the next half-century, however, rising numbers of black slaves created strong pressures toward racial solidarity among whites of all social classes, while a steady expansion of the economy eased serious economic tensions within the mostly rural and free white population. Under these conditions, the lower and middling ranks of that population became more and more willing to accept the leadership of the colony's increasingly wealthy and visible elite.

With little resistance from the rest of the free population, members of the elite eagerly took on the political and social obligations appropriate to their status. They dominated civil and religious institutions at both the local and provincial levels and took pride in being responsive to the wishes of their constituents. In the process, they helped to give the colony's political system enormously more energy, stability, and authority than it had ever exhibited during its first century of existence.

These tendencies were fostered by Britain's chief representative in the colony, Lieutenant Governor Sir William Gooch, who held office from 1727 to 1749. In contrast to several of his predecessors, Gooch took great pains to cultivate and work in cooperation with the local gentry.

By casting himself in the role of a "patriot" governor who always put the good of the country above his own private interests and trying through his own behavior to provide an example of responsible, dedicated, and disinterested public leadership, Gooch sought with astonishing success to encourage Virginia political leaders to adopt the same goals and behave in the same fashion. Simultaneously, he publicly encouraged the people at large to defer to their gentry leaders and emphasized the importance of harmony and moderation in public life.

With the cooperation of leading local politicians including John Holloway, Sir John Randolph, and John Robinson, the three men who held the office of speaker of the House of Burgesses during his administration, Gooch, by these means, fashioned a previously unknown political stability that remained intact for the rest of the colonial period. So common during the seventeenth and early eighteenth centuries, tumult in public life became rare and political factions disappeared.

Unlike their counterparts in several other colonies, Virginia legislators routinely supported Gooch and his administration. Although controversies between governors and legislatures were common to British colonial government, after 1720 Virginia experienced only one such episode during the early 1750s. Increasingly, Virginia acquired a reputation as Britain's most loyal and politically moderate American colony, and its leaders took special pride in that reputation.

During the fifty years immediately prior to the American Revolution, in fact, Virginia enjoyed a degree of public harmony and political tranquility that contrasted sharply both with its own past and with the experience of all but a few of Britain's other American colonies. Virginia politics became a classic example of what one scholar has described as a situation of traditional stability.

In the absence of large or important towns, with overall economic prosperity, with few colony-wide political issues to politicize the electorate, and without serious social divisions among the free population, the countryside was dominant and the rural elite governed without serious challenge. The tenantry and yeomanry assumed an only marginally active role in politics, and the small class of merchants and lawyers allied itself with the dominant plantation elite.

Robert Carter of Cleve and his wife, Ann, were members of the gentry class.

Under these conditions, politics became a highly respected avocation for members of the elite. Earlier generations had fulfilled themselves by acquiring landed estates, enhancing the family name, and obtaining status and wealth in the community. But their extraordinary success in realizing these ambitions meant that members of the generation that came into manhood after 1720 had to look elsewhere to satisfy their desire to excel.

More and more through the middle decades of the eighteenth century, the sons and grandsons of the founding fathers of the Virginia gentry discovered that politics was the most exciting and challenging activity in the life of rural Virginia, and the more ambitious among them entered into public life with the same energy that their ancestors had shown in carving out a place for their families in the New World.

As politics increasingly became the primary road to fame in Virginia society after 1720, the colony's political system gradually assumed a well-defined shape. Politics came to operate within a set of well-established and well-understood institutions, traditions, conventions, and assumptions that will be explained below.

Local Governance

Unlike the situation in modern America, the most important units of government in colonial Virginia were those that operated on the local level. Almost from the colony's beginnings, Virginia's political life had been centered in the counties. By 1728, there were already thirty counties in Virginia, and the number increased to fifty-four over the next thirty-five years.

This 1724 drawing shows the Northhampton County courthouse. Note the gallows just to the right of the courthouse.
Courtesy, Northhampton County Courthouse.

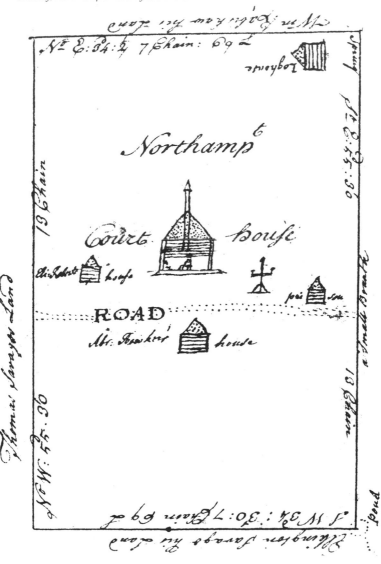

In Virginia as in England, a county court, composed of all of the justices of the peace in the county, was the chief agency of government. The number of these "gentlemen justices," or magistrates, ranged from fifteen to thirty, and the public at large had no voice in their selection. Rather, in the English tradition, they were appointed by the king's governor with the advice of his Council. Although other influential people sometimes successfully recommended appointees to the governor and Council, the courts themselves nominated the overwhelming majority of the new justices. As a result, they were virtually self-perpetuating bodies.

These local magistracies always included a large proportion of the wealthy and prominent men in the county. Talented and successful immigrants often gained appointment. By the mid-eighteenth century in the older counties of eastern Virginia, however, all but a few magistrates came from families that had been long-established in the county and were so closely interrelated through several generations of intermarriage that they constituted one large "tangled cousinry."

Over time, as members of the county magistracies became ever more tightly interconnected through family and kinship ties, the courts became more and more oligarchic. That is, they became less open to men who were not closely related to the county's dominant families.

If membership on the county courts was increasingly concentrated in the hands of a few influential families, the power of the courts over local affairs was great and was formally subject to control only from the provincial government at Williamsburg. Like the justices themselves, a few local officeholders—the county sheriff, coroner, militia officers, and tobacco inspectors—were appointed by the royal governor, while the county clerk was appointed by the secretary of the colony. But the county courts directly appointed most other local officers, including constables and surveyors of roads. Not a single local civil or judicial officer was elected.

Nor was the situation much different in the ecclesiastical realm. The Anglican church was the established church throughout Virginia prior to 1785, which meant that it was supported by public taxes that all taxpayers, regardless of their religious preferences, were required to pay. Most counties were divided into two or more parishes, and each parish was presided over by a twelve-man vestry that had responsibility for building and maintaining churches, employing ministers, making sure that property boundaries were understood, and administering poor relief.

Composed of the same types of people who were justices of the peace, the vestries were originally elected by the freeholders and householders of the parish. Following this initial election, however, the vestries themselves had power to appoint new members. Although custom probably prevented most vestries from going against the opinion of their parishioners in the election of new vestrymen, local voters could not elect a wholly new vestry without an act of the Virginia legislature.

In civil affairs, the courts not only had broad appointive powers, they were also responsible for all local administrative and judicial matters. They met monthly to set tax rates, issue tavern licenses, supervise the upkeep of roads, bridges, and ferries, and oversee the administration of land transfers, estates of the deceased, and the care of all unfortunates. They also had authority to enforce order and punish violations of community social norms.

In this last task, they had the assistance of the grand jury. A group of lesser freeholders chosen by the court, this body met annually to identify public officials who were neglecting their duties and to single out other local residents who were guilty of violations of the colony's moral code. These included missing church, swearing, drunkenness, fornication, adultery, bastardy, vagrancy, disturbing the peace, and tax evasion. The courts also dealt with all criminal violations, including slave felonies, though they usually sent more serious criminal offenders to Williamsburg to be tried by the General Court, the supreme court of Virginia.

Such extensive power carried with it extraordinarily heavy responsibilities. To an important degree, the peace, good order, and general welfare of the counties depended on how well the courts performed their specific duties. At the end of the seventeenth century, educated English immigrants had complained about "the Insufficiency of these Courts." They charged that most of the "Country Gentlemen" who served as justices "had no Education in the Law." Having "been born in *Virginia*," few of the justices, according to these critics, had had any "Opportunity of Improvement by good Education, further than they learn to read, write, and cast Accompts, and that but very indifferently."

Although this situation may have improved somewhat during the first quarter of the eighteenth century, Lieutenant Gov-

The Hanover County courthouse still looks much as it did in the eighteenth century.

ernor Gooch made a concerted effort during his long tenure to impress upon the justices the importance of their role in local governance and to encourage them to make themselves masters of the law and, in the best tradition of gentlemen magistrates in England, to think of themselves as men of "Substance and Ability . . . and Estate" who were required by their position in society to assume the weighty responsibilities of providing their respective localities with the best possible government.

Under Gooch's sponsorship, George Webb, himself a justice in New Kent County, prepared a detailed handbook designed to inform justices how to conduct themselves in office. Entitled *The Office and Authority of a Justice of the Peace* and published in Williamsburg in 1736, this volume also spelled out the desired qualifications for the office.

16

According to Webb, justices were supposed to be, above all, able and God-fearing men of ample fortune and "known Loialty to the King" who were devoted to the preservation of "the Peace and good Government of their Country." Though they were certainly expected to have sufficient knowledge of the law to enable them to "execute their Office and Authority to the Advancement of Justice . . . and without Reproach to themselves," legal learning was far less important than several specific personal characteristics.

Thus, in their private lives, justices were to be people "of the best Reputation, good Governance, and Courage for the Truth." No less significant, they were to be hardworking and willing to sacrifice their own "private Emploiment, or Ease" to the demands of public office.

Most important of all, they were supposed to be "Lovers of Justice." Enjoined by their oaths of office to "do equal Right to all Manner of People, Great and Small, High and Low, Rich and Poor, according to Equity, good Conscience, and the Laws and Usages of the Colony," they were expected to act "without

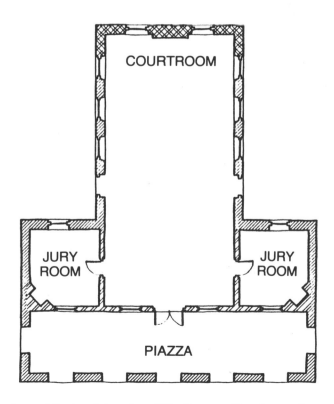

An architectural drawing of the Hanover County courthouse.

Eighteenth-century Virginians were urged to "Keep Within Compass."

Favour, Affection, or Partiality" and always to be dedicated to represent "the Benefit of the People" at large and not the narrow interests of themselves or people from their own class.

By associating the office of justice of the peace with such high standards, Gooch successfully tried to raise the status of the office. Thereafter, for a man to be appointed to a justiceship meant that he had been identified as a person who, at least to some degree, met those standards. The honor, prestige, and self-esteem that derived from the office help to explain why through the middle decades of the eighteenth century it was sought so eagerly by the sons of the gentry.

But these benefits were at least partially offset by the major commitment of time and energy it required. A diligent justice could spend from twenty to forty days a year on court business, and the burden was particularly heavy for members of the quorum, a select group of justices in each county singled out because of their special legal or other knowledge. The presence of at least one member of the quorum was necessary at all judicial proceedings. No justice received any pay or other direct material rewards for this heavy investment of time.

That many of the wealthiest and most talented men in Virginia were willing to undertake such a burdensome office without pay may seem puzzling to modern-day Americans. In doing so, however, Virginians were behaving in a way that had the sanction of a long tradition that stretched back to ancient Greece and Rome. Today most Americans believe that public office should be open to all people regardless of social class, wealth, education, or family background. But colonial Virginians had more traditional notions of public affairs.

According to those notions, the happiness of every political society depended, in the words of one Anglican minister in 1776, "in great measure, on the well ordering of society," and order, in turn, depended upon a necessary "subordination in society." However complex the economic and social divisions, there were, according to traditional conceptions, only two groups in politics: the governed and the governors.

The governed consisted of virtually everybody in the middling and lower ranks of people, most of whom had to spend so much time earning a living for themselves and their families that they lacked both the time and the opportunity to acquire the special knowledge and ability that were thought to be necessary for all but the lowliest of public offices.

Far from aspiring to a major role in politics, such people were expected to live honest, God-fearing, industrious, and predominantly private lives while playing only a subordinate role in public affairs. As Governor Gooch put it in the early 1730s, they were supposed to stick to their own business, make good tobacco, shun those "given to Noise and Violence," and "Submit . . . to every Law." The welfare of Virginia, declared the Reverend James Horrocks, president of the College of William and Mary, in 1763, required that the broad body of the people pay "a dutiful Obedience to the Laws of our Country, and those of [our] Superiors, who have the Care of them."

By contrast, the governors were composed of those few people who by virtue of their socioeconomic position supposedly had the time and the necessary qualifications to assume the role of political superiors. By and large, Virginians did not believe that the gentry had an "exclusive Title to Common Sense, Wisdom or Integrity."

But most free people seem to have acknowledged that the gentry did have what one writer referred to as the "solid and splendid Advantages of Education and Accomplishments; extensive Influence, and incitement to Glory," the very qualities, it was widely assumed, that best fitted men to "assume the Character of Politicians." Because they also had "a greater Stake in the Country" and enjoyed a "larger Property," members of the gentry were supposedly also, as the Reverend William Stith of the College claimed in 1752, "bound . . . to be more studious of that Country's Good."

If most free Virginians seem to have accepted the principle that the governing class should be limited to "Gentlemen and Persons of Distinction," they also believed that such men were obliged to assume the burdens of government. As the natural leaders of their society, they were expected through the example of their "Lives and Conversations" to lead "the Generality of the People" to be virtuous and honest citizens. Through their steady and impartial devotion to public service, they were also supposed to make sure that the people understood and obeyed the laws and that government operated efficiently and fairly.

That there was a considerable disparity between these ideals and the reality of governance in Virginia is scarcely surprising. Despite Gooch's efforts to stimulate justices and other local officials to achieve a higher level of performance, few justices actually met the lofty standards prescribed in Webb's handbook.

Throughout the eighteenth century, there were complaints about the quality of local government. Some people protested that there were insufficient checks upon the powers of the justices, that there were no safeguards to insure that they were not "byasst by Interest to themselves or perticular friends," or that they had too little legal knowledge to discharge their judicial duties with competence.

Never known for their unreserved respect for authority, local freeholders occasionally even showed their contempt for a particular court by brazen insults. An especially dramatic example occurred in Richmond County in March 1771 when the justices found upon entering court that the bench upon which they sat had been daubed "with Tar and Dung in many places" in obvious contempt of the court's authority.

Yet, notwithstanding such occasional displays of public discontent, the people at large seem not to have been unhappy with existing political arrangements on the local level. Retaining a high degree of trust in their justices, ordinary Virginians continued throughout the last half-century of the colonial era to accept the role of the magistrates as the chief interpreters and enforcers of law and morality in the counties. Prior to the late 1760s, there was neither any widespread challenge to the authority of the justices nor any serious demand for fundamental change in the system.

Perhaps the primary reason for the widespread public acceptance of this increasingly oligarchic system lay in the fact that the justices seem to have been broadly responsive to the wishes of local freeholders. They may not have been elected by the public. But it was a commonplace among contemporary political thinkers that "government was founded on opinion." What theorists meant by that phrase was that no government could function successfully without the support of the governed.

Involved in continuous interaction with the broad body of freeholders in their localities, Virginia justices were acutely aware that public acceptance of their authority and the stability of local government depended upon their acting in ways that would not meet with the disapproval of the larger community of freeholders. If the freeholders demonstrated an astonishing amount of deference to county magistrates, it was thus to a major extent because the magistrates were careful not to act in ways that would be annoying to the freeholders.

Elections

On the local level, political life in colonial Virginia thus provided little scope for direct participation by the general public. In Virginia, as in eighteenth-century Britain, the only occasions when ordinary citizens had a formal voice in the political process were elections of representatives to the lower house of the legislature.

Each county sent two representatives to the House of Burgesses, while the towns of Jamestown, Williamsburg, and Norfolk and the College of William and Mary each sent one. All representatives were selected at a poll of eligible voters. In contrast to the modern American political system, by no means all of the adult inhabitants of any county or town were eligible to vote.

With regard to voting eligibility, Virginia did not depart radically from contemporary British theory, according to which voting was limited to those who could meet two tests. First, they had to be independent and not dependent. In the language of the time, they could not be subject to the will of any other man. Thus all dependents including children, wives, servants, slaves, adult males who had insufficient property to make them independent, and Catholics, who were thought to be dependent upon the Pope in Rome, were excluded from voting.

Second, to be qualified to vote, individuals had to be able to control their own passions, a requirement that eliminated whole categories of people thought by the dominant segment of the population to lack the capacity for self-control. These included unmarried women and supposedly uncivilized groups such as free blacks, Indians, criminals, and the insane.

In effect, voting was thus confined to white Protestant males twenty-one years of age or older who were in possession (either through outright ownership or a long-term lease) of sufficient property to make them independent. As defined by the Virginia election law of 1736, the amount of property required was either one hundred acres of unimproved land, twenty-five acres of improved land with a house on it, or a town lot with a house on it. Men could vote in every county in which they met the property requirement.

The best modern estimates suggest that about one-fifth of the white inhabitants were adult males. Of them, perhaps as many as eighty to ninety percent eventually acquired enough property during their lifetimes to qualify them to vote. As restricted as these figures appear by today's standards, they were extremely liberal in comparison with eighteenth-century Britain, where in many counties no more than fifteen to twenty percent of adult white males had enough property to enable them to vote in elections for members of the House of Commons.

Elections occurred irregularly in colonial Virginia. By law they had to be held at least once every seven years, but the royal lieutenant governors, whose responsibility it was to call elections, had wide discretion in deciding how often and when Virginians would go to the polls.

Between 1695 and 1720, elections took place on an average of once every two and one-quarter years. But thereafter the average time between elections almost doubled to four years. Between 1720 and 1766, a period of forty-six years, there were only ten elections. Two in 1769 and others in 1772 and 1775 meant that elections were somewhat more frequent during the troubled years of crisis that preceded the American Revolution.

Elections in eighteenth-century England were raucous affairs.

Perhaps because they were so infrequent, elections tended to be gala events. They were usually held at the county courthouse on a regular court day. Often located at a dirt crossroads in a still heavily forested area with only a crude inn and a few houses in the immediate vicinity, Virginia court-houses were usually quiet and virtually deserted. But they came alive on monthly court days, which throughout the colony served as occasions for social diversion and business transactions. Like the occasional militia musters, elections drew large crowds of people as voters poured in from the farthest reaches of the county.

Although the law required all eligible voters to vote, the turnout was rarely much over fifty percent except when a major issue was at stake or when there was an intense rivalry among candidates. In more populous counties, even a small turnout could mean from three hundred to six hundred voters, a very large congregation of people for a rural society like colonial Virginia.

Presided over by the county sheriff, elections usually lasted for a whole day and sometimes even continued into a second. They were not conducted by secret ballot. Rather, like Englishmen in Britain itself, Virginians voted *viva voce*—each voter declared his choices out loud in front of the sheriff, the various candidates, and the rest of the people in attendance.

No less than contemporary Englishmen, colonial Virginians prided themselves on this system of open voting. They believed that honorable and courageous men should not be afraid to stand up and express their opinions publicly and that such a system was far less liable to fraud than election by secret ballot. Because every county had two representatives, each voter could choose two candidates, and a staff of clerks (usually one for each candidate) recorded his preferences. After everyone had voted, the sheriff closed the poll. Following a tally of the votes, he then declared the two candidates with the highest totals elected.

Some candidates were so popular that nobody bothered to oppose them, but most elections seem to have been contested. The number vying for the two seats sometimes was as high as ten to twelve, although three to five was the more usual number of candidates. By law, any voter could put himself up as a candidate; by custom, only those who could lay claim to the status of gentlemen usually did so. The costs of "standing for burgess" (running for election) were far too expensive for most men.

Custom kept men from campaigning openly, and the law strictly forbade candidates from "treating" or otherwise endeavoring to "buy" the favor of voters. In actual fact, however, "swilling the planters with bumbo" (an alcoholic punch) was an accepted election practice, and candidates often sought to woo votes by giving preelection barbecues and other lavish entertainments.

Supposedly the friends of a candidate supplied the liquor and food for these events, but the candidate himself usually wound up paying for them. Some victorious candidates even gave postelection dinners and balls. George Washington spent as much as £50 on an election, a sum that few men in any county could afford.

If money was essential for the successful candidate, so also was support from the local gentry. In deciding which candidates to support, the gentry were rarely unanimous, but they usually agreed on what kinds of men they did not want to represent the county in Williamsburg.

In general, they did not back gamblers, drunks, spendthrifts, and others who fell into the category of what one Anglican minister derisively referred to as "decayed Gentry." Nor did they usually prefer social upstarts, the "Ass-queers" who, having suddenly acquired a visible estate, insisted upon attaching the term "Esquire" to their names despite the fact that they lacked the learning and gentility associated with that title.

Not that the eighteenth-century Virginia gentry had anything against wealth, newly gained or otherwise. But in selecting representatives they considered other qualities to be far more important. The official writs issued by the lieutenant governor to the county sheriffs empowering them to hold an election commanded the voters to choose two of the "most fit and able Men" of the county to represent them, and George Webb's manual for justices urged voters to pick "Persons of Knowledge, Integrity, Courage, Probity, Loialty, and Experience, without Regard to Personal Inclination or Prejudice."

To a remarkable degree, local gentry groups seem to have taken such prescriptions seriously. In Virginia, a young New Jersey tutor discovered in the early 1770s that the man who was "best esteemed and most applauded" was the one who attended "to his business . . . with the greatest diligence." And it was not only diligence but a whole cluster of related qualities—honesty and liberality, moderation and humility, courage and impartiality, learning and judgment, circumspection and frugality—that recommended a man to his neighborhood peers.

Wealth and local gentry support were not in themselves enough to gain the favor of the voters. To be sure, after 1720 the voters rarely chose anyone to represent them who did not have local gentry backing and was not himself a gentleman. No matter how impressive their other qualities, however, few candidates could expect success if they were personally disagreeable to the broad body of voters. Ultimately, their vastly superior numbers dictated that they, and not the gentry, would be the ones who made the choice.

If candidates did not always, as one contemporary critic of the Virginia electoral system charged, have to resign their "reason, and be nought but what each voter pleases," they were nonetheless always at the mercy of "the humours of a fickle crowd." Only the most secure candidate did not find it necessary to "lower" himself a little to gain election. Any man who was arrogant, haughty, condescending, or inaccessible in his relations with the local electorate had little chance of winning.

The most revealing contemporary account of colonial Virginia voting behavior is to be found in a play written in 1770 entitled *The Candidates: or, the Humours of a Virginia Election*. Written by Robert Munford, sometime sheriff and burgess for Mecklenburg County, *The Candidates* was a three-act comedy that revolved around the efforts of a fictional county to choose its two burgesses.

In the previous legislature it had been represented by two men of the sort Virginians were supposed to elect. *Worthy* was a gentleman of unquestionable distinction who took pride in having "[n]ever courted the people for the troublesome office they have hitherto imposed upon me," while *Wou'dbe,* a man of somewhat lesser accomplishments and standing, was nonetheless "a clever civil gentleman . . . of . . . good learning" who knew "the punctilios of behaving himself, with the best of them." Because *Worthy* had declined to run again, three new men entered the race. *Sir John Toddy,* "an honest blockhead" and good-natured old sot, was obviously one of Virginia's "decayed Gentry." *Strutabout* and *Smallhopes* were a pair of ignorant and ostentatious social upstarts who sought to secure votes by keeping "the liquor . . . running."

In the early going, the voters seemed to be most favorably disposed to *Strutabout* and *Smallhopes,* who attempted to discredit *Worthy* by spreading lies about his behavior during his earlier terms in the House of Burgesses and promised to do whatever the voters asked. By contrast, *Wou'dbe*, obviously the best of the four candidates, would make no promises and, as one freeholder remarked, "did not love diversion enough." He was on the verge of going down to defeat when *Worthy*, angered by the actions of *Strutabout* and *Smallhopes*, changed his mind and entered the lists in alliance with *Wou'dbe*.

Despite the fact that *Worthy* chided them for having, "for the sake of a little toddy, . . . behave[d] in a manner so contradictory to the candour and integrity which always should prevail among mankind," the voters immediately gave their support to the two obviously superior candidates, who won the election handily. *Wou'dbe* thereupon congratulated the voters for having shown their good "judgment, and a spirit of independence becoming Virginians," while one of their number, *Captain Paunch*, declared proudly that they had indeed "done as we ought, we have elected the ablest, according to the writ."

In *The Candidates*, Munford was trying to *prescribe* how an election should turn out rather than to *describe* one that actually happened. Obviously inspired by instances in which the voters had not voted for "the ablest," the play was intended to recall them to a proper sense of their responsibilities.

With liquor flowing so freely and candidates often competing fiercely with one another, elections could become heated affairs in which, contrary to Virginia ideals of what should be, passion overcame reason and men of inferior ability gained election. One critic charged that voters all too often measured "the merits of a Candidate" entirely "by the number of his treats" and put far more emphasis upon "the quantities of his beef and brandy" than upon "his integrity or sense." Others complained that voters were frequently taken in by outlandish promises.

As a rule, however, Virginia voters seem to have borne out the judgment of the contemporary Scottish philosopher David Hume. The middling and "lower sort[s] of people and small proprietors," Hume noted, were "good judges enough of one not very distant from them" and could therefore usually be expected to "chuse the best, or nearly the best representative[s]."

If by generous treating or excessive promises, men of small talents occasionally carried an election, the broader electorate was not unmindful of the same considerations that impressed the gentry. Good character, an easy and open manner,

Edmund Pendleton.

diligence, outstanding ability, and public spirit were the qualities they usually seem to have looked for in a candidate, and
only those of considerable merit could expect to continue to
enjoy the long-term support of their constituents.

"From the experience of nearly sixty years in public life,"
Edmund Pendleton, one of the foremost lawyers in Virginia and
a powerful figure in provincial and state politics, wrote in 1798,
"I have been taught to . . . respect this my native country for the
decent, peaceable, and orderly behaviour of its inhabitants;
justice has been, and is duly and diligently administered—the
laws obeyed—the constituted authorities respected, and we
have lived in the happy intercourse of private harmony and
good will. At the same time by a free communication between
those of more information on political subjects and the classes
who have not otherwise an opportunity of acquiring that knowledge, all were instructed in their *rights* and *duties* as freemen,
and taught to respect them."

Provincial Administration

When a man left his county to go to the capitol in Williamsburg to serve in the General Assembly, he was heading into a very different world. In the counties, the authority of Britain as well as that of the provincial government in Williamsburg was usually rather remote. Local officials acted in the name of the British monarch and on the basis of the king's commission issued by his representative in Williamsburg. For all practical purposes, however, the local gentry serving as justices of the peace governed the counties with minimal interference from Williamsburg.

By contrast, the world of Williamsburg revolved around the king's representative in Virginia. In most royal colonies, the king was represented by a royal governor in chief. For most of the eighteenth century, however, the governorship of Virginia was a lucrative sinecure for a royal favorite, usually a member of the British nobility, who never came to the colony. A sinecure was an office that permitted the person who held it to collect a substantial proportion of the financial benefits of the office while the duties were performed by a deputy.

Only at the very end of the colonial period during the last stages of the crisis that led to the American Revolution did two

The legislature of the Virginia colony met in the Capitol at Williamsburg.

of Virginia's royal governors—Norborne Berkeley, Baron de Botetourt (1768–1770) and John Murray, fourth Earl of Dunmore (1771–1775)—actually reside in the colony.

For the previous sixty-three years, the colony was administered by a series of lieutenant governors: Edward Nott (1705–1706), Alexander Spotswood (1710–1722), Hugh Drysdale (1722–1726), William Gooch (1727–1749), Robert Dinwiddie (1751–1758), and Francis Fauquier (1758–1768). Although they lived in the governor's elegant and imposing palace in the center of Williamsburg and had all of the authority and responsibilities of the governorship, these lieutenant governors received only half of the salary and fees arising from the office.

As the embodiment of royal authority in Virginia and as the most direct formal link between the colony and Britain, the lieutenant governor or, after 1768, the governor had enormous prestige and immense potential influence. Delegated to him by the king in a royal commission issued at the time of his appointment, the governor's formal authority was extensive.

He was responsible for administering the government and making sure that laws were duly executed. His consent was necessary for all legislation, and he presided over the General Court in its judicial proceedings. The head of the established church and commander in chief of all military and naval forces, he theoretically had the power to appoint all ministers and military and civil officers.

In practice, however, the lieutenant governor's appointive powers were far more limited than they seemed on paper. In Britain during the early eighteenth century, the king's leading ministers had built effective political machines through the careful use of the crown's powers of appointment. By a judicious distribution of profitable offices among potential supporters in Parliament, Sir Robert Walpole, who served as the king's chief minister for over two decades beginning in the early 1720s, created an extensive system of patronage that attached a majority of the most prominent political leaders from both the House of Lords and the House of Commons to the king.

Walpole thereby insured the ministry that such beneficiaries of the king's largesse would throw their weight behind government measures in Parliament. This "court" interest proved to be the basis for Britain's remarkable political stability through almost the whole of the eighteenth century.

None of Virginia's chief executives was able to duplicate this system in the colony. At the provincial level, there were simply too few offices to provide them with much patronage. By modern standards, the executive arm of the government was exceedingly small. It consisted of only twelve major officials, each of whom had only a handful of clerks to assist him.

A secretary kept the colony's records. An attorney general was responsible for law enforcement. A receiver general collected the small rents charged by the crown for all lands and all other royal revenues. Six naval officers, scattered widely over the colony, collected customs duties and oversaw the enforcement of British trade regulations. An auditor general examined and audited all accounts of revenues collected by the receiver general and customs officials. A treasurer was in charge of collecting all taxes levied by the Virginia legislature.

Except for the treasurer, who was chosen by an act of the legislature, these twelve officers were all appointed directly by the crown's ministers in Britain. They in turn appointed their own clerks and other subordinate officers. Including these lesser officers, the entire provincial bureaucracy did not exceed forty to fifty men, not a single one of whom was appointed exclusively by the lieutenant governor.

Nor did the chief executive have much more patronage at the local level. In theory, he had the authority to appoint most important local officers. But by custom most of the officers, including the sheriff, justice of the peace, and tobacco inspectors, went to the nominees of the county courts and prominent local gentry.

Unlike the situation in Britain, then, the influence of the resident governor in Virginia depended not on patronage but on his ability to provide effective and persuasive public leadership and to perform his duties in a way the society approved. Some of them—Drysdale, Gooch, Fauquier, and Botetourt—were enormously successful in this effort, while others—Spotswood, Dinwiddie, and Dunmore—acted early in their governorships in ways that made Virginians suspicious and never managed to establish their moral authority over the public affairs of the colony.

The royal lieutenant governor may not have had a large group of subordinate officials to provide him with an extensive base of political support, but he could usually count on the twelve members of his advisory Council for assistance. Like the governor, they were appointed by the crown in Britain and could be removed whenever the crown saw fit. For all practical purposes, however, they served for life. The fact that their appointments came directly from the king was sufficient to bring councillors great political prestige within the colony. Many councillors also held one of the major executive offices described above.

Because it was the most honorific position to which most Virginians could aspire and because the salary was considerable, a Council seat was much prized. A few wealthy or well-connected men from newer families such as the brothers William and Thomas Nelson from Yorktown sometimes gained appointments, and the commissary for the Anglican church, the chief ecclesiastical officer in the Virginia religious establishment, usually held one of the seats.

But the body was dominated by members of the colony's old elite families. At one time or another during the four decades preceding the American Revolution, seats were held by two different members each of the Burwell, Byrd, Carter, Corbin, Fairfax, Lee, and Tayloe families and one each of the Beverley, Custis, Grymes, Lightfoot, Lewis, Page, Thornton, Randolph, and Wormeley families.

The General Court held its sessions in this elaborate chamber.

Although the Council's actual power gradually declined after the early decades of the eighteenth century when it helped to unseat at least two governors, the visibility and connections of its members insured that the Council would continue to command considerable influence in Virginia political life.

The Council also had considerable formal authority. Specifically, it had three separate and very important functions. First, as the upper house of the General Assembly, the Virginia equivalent of the British House of Lords, its consent was required to all legislation. Second, as the General Court, it was the supreme judicial tribunal and the last court of appeal in Virginia. Third, and most important, as the lieutenant governor's chief advisory body, it counseled him on all administrative and executive matters and its president, the most senior member in terms of date of appointment, acted as chief executive whenever the royal lieutenant governor was out of the colony or if he died.

In all of these functions, the Council was expected by officials in Britain to join with the lieutenant governor in upholding British authority in the colony. Councillors did not have to reside in Williamsburg. But because the Council met so frequently, a majority usually lived either close by or no farther than a day's ride from the capital.

The House of Burgesses and the Development of Political Leadership

Because the executive arm was so small and the Council had only twelve members, a seat in the House of Burgesses was the only opportunity available for the vast majority of Virginians who aspired to a political career in the provincial government. By the 1770s, there were 126 representatives, nearly two and a half times the number of men serving in the executive branch.

Whenever the governor summoned the General Assembly to meet in Williamsburg, the sudden influx of burgesses, many of whom were accompanied by servants and wives, along with the many other people who had business with the legislature greatly increased the normally slow pace of life in the colonial capital. Inns quickly filled up, and many burgesses had to find accommodations in private houses. Intermixed with the business of the legislature was a round of glittering parties and dances at the Governor's Palace and in the homes of councillors and other prominent local inhabitants.

Legislative sessions were usually short. Depending upon the amount of business to be done, they could last from a few days to several weeks. Only in wartime or in very unusual situations did the General Assembly meet for more than thirty to forty days in any given year. Indeed, in some years it did not meet at all.

Notwithstanding the fact that it was only infrequently in session, the House of Burgesses had significant power. As the branch of the legislature most closely tied to the inhabitants of Virginia, it took the leading role in passing laws. Through a series of standing and temporary committees it considered the petitions and grievances that came to the legislature from the localities as well as all proposals made by members for passing new laws or amending old ones.

In the tradition of the British House of Commons, it was the only branch of government that could initiate any taxes to be levied on the inhabitants. Perhaps most important, in the same tradition, it was thought to be the primary guardian of those precious rights and privileges Virginians had brought with them from Britain. "One of the main Fundamentals of our Constitution," the House of Burgesses, as one contemporary remarked, was "the chief Support of the Liberty and Property of the Subject," the bulwark against oppression of the free inhabitants by their rulers.

Along with the governor and Council, it was responsible for calling corrupt, rapacious, or arbitrary local officials to account, standing up to those wicked or misguided members of the executive branch who exceeded their rightful powers, and petitioning for redress of grievances suffered by the colony as a result of actions by the government in Britain.

At least in part because of its growing size and prestige, the House of Burgesses after 1720 rapidly supplanted the Council as the more powerful branch of the legislature. As the main arena of political action for those eager to gain fame in public life, it served as the advanced training ground for that galaxy of talented politicians who made such an important contribution to the American Revolution and founding of the United States.

Within the House, the pinnacle of success was election to the speakership. Though he had to be approved by the chief executive, the speaker was chosen by his fellow burgesses at the first meeting of the legislature following each new election.

Throughout the eighteenth century, the speaker of the British House of Commons retained a close association with the

A View of the House of Commons.

B. Cole. sculp.

The Virginia House of Burgesses was modeled on the British House of Commons.

crown and was, in effect, almost as much an agent for the crown as the servant of the House. By contrast, the Virginia speaker was both the most popular figure in the House and its political leader.

As the highest elected official in Virginia, the speaker's influence reached far beyond the walls of the House. With the single exception of the governor, he was the most powerful figure in the entire Virginia political establishment. Moreover, from 1692 to 1715 and from 1723 to 1766, he also served as treasurer of Virginia, a post that brought him a commission of four to five percent on all taxes collected as a result of legislative levies in the colony.

The speaker's formal power was substantial. Seated on a raised podium in front of the House, he determined what matters would be brought before the House at what time, regulated debate, and appointed the members to all committees, including the influential heads of the House's five standing committees on privileges and elections, petitions and grievances, courts of justice, trade, and religion.

Because he was the presiding officer of the House, he could not speak in debate. But he could make his opinions known simply by transforming the House into a committee of the whole and appointing one of his colleagues to take the chair. Although all matters within the House were determined by majority vote, the opinion of the speaker almost always carried enormous weight with most of the other members.

For twenty-eight years between his first election in 1738 and his death in 1766, the speaker was John Robinson of King and Queen County, a central tidewater county on the peninsula between the York and Rappahannock rivers. The son of a prominent gentry family, Robinson first took a seat in the House of Burgesses in 1727, the same year that Lieutenant Governor Gooch arrived in the colony. He quickly became the protégé of Gooch and of Sir John Randolph, his predecessor as speaker. During his long tenure in office, Robinson acquired such extraordinary political popularity that by the early 1760s he could be described by Lieutenant Governor Fauquier as the very "Darling of the Country."

Robinson's enormous popularity and power derived in part from the "weight and influence" of the "Speaker's . . . Chair" among those who were "candidates for his countenance and favour." In part, it also resulted, as was discovered after his death, from his liberal distribution to his associates and support-

John Robinson.

ers of unsecured loans from public funds entrusted to him as treasurer.

But Robinson's popularity and influence were much too general to be explained entirely in such terms. Far more important were his "sound political knowledge," his public character as a man of "great integrity, assiduity, and ability in business," and his personification of the politics of prudence and restraint so much admired by the gentry. No less important was his extraordinary warmth of personality, "a benevolence which created friends and a sincerity which never lost one." These personal qualities won for him widespread applause and admiration as "a jewil of a man" whose "opinions must [always] be regarded."

Robinson invariably impressed contemporaries with his "acquaintance with parliamentary forms" and the grace with which he filled the speaker's chair. "When he presided," one Virginian proudly recalled after Robinson's death, "the decorum of the house outshone that [even] of the British House of Commons. . . . When he propounded a question, his comprehension and perspicuity brought it equally to the most humble and the most polished understanding. To committees he nominated the members best qualified. He stated to the House the contents of every bill and showed himself to be a perfect master of the subject. When he pronounced the rules of order, he convinced the reluctant. When on the floor of a committee of the whole house, he opened the debate, he submitted resolutions and enforced them with simplicity and might. In the limited sphere of colonial politics, he was a column."

During Robinson's long tenure as speaker, the House of Burgesses first began to develop that broad range and depth of political talent that Virginia would exhibit in so much abundance during the Revolutionary era. Among Robinson's own political generation, men who were born within ten or twelve years before or after his birth in 1704, were a number of men of impressive learning and legislative ability.

They included Sir John Randolph, Robinson's immediate predecessor as speaker; Richard Bland, a noted lawyer, antiquarian, and pamphleteer; Charles Carter of Cleve and Landon Carter, accomplished and public-spirited planter sons of Robert "King" Carter, the richest man in Virginia at the time of his death in 1732; the two Nelson brothers, William, the merchant, and Thomas, the lawyer, both of whom became councillors; Edward Barradall, James Power, Benjamin Waller, and Beverley Whiting, four of the best-known Virginia lawyers of their generation; and William Beverley, George Braxton, Jr., Carter Burwell, Henry Fitzhugh, Benjamin Harrison IV, and Philip Ludwell, all tidewater planters whose strong political interests and abilities brought them to the top of the leadership of the House.

Bringing their experience in local government with them to the legislature, these men first entered the House of Burgesses between 1727 and 1752 at ages ranging from twenty-three to forty-two, the average being around thirty-two. In contrast to earlier generations of Virginia legislators, they had long careers that usually lasted until their deaths. Robinson was in the House for thirty-nine years, Bland for thirty-four, and Charles Carter for thirty. The most prominent House members of Robinson's generation served for an average of fourteen years, and only those who died young or were appointed to the Council served for fewer than eleven years.

Like Virginia political leaders of earlier generations, they were predominantly planters, but nearly half were lawyers. All of them had either died or retired by the mid-1770s, and only Bland, Landon Carter, Thomas Nelson, and Waller played a significant role in the troubles preceding the American Revolution.

If few members of Robinson's political generation survived long enough to take an active part in the great events of the Revolutionary era, they were the teachers of the men who did. From the late 1740s on, they were passing their accumulated political expertise on to a second generation of political leaders, which included most of the men who distinguished themselves in the service of Virginia and the United States between 1760 and 1800.

Born within eight to ten years on either side of 1725, this younger generation consisted of those who entered political life during the two decades prior to the Revolution and began to assume a large role in public affairs in the late 1750s or 1760s. By the mid-1760s, political leadership in Virginia had largely passed into their hands.

The most prominent member of this new generation was Attorney General Peyton Randolph. Son of former speaker Sir John Randolph, he succeeded Robinson as speaker in 1766 and became president of the First Continental Congress in 1774. Like Randolph, a majority of the leaders of this generation were attorneys. Edmund Pendleton, Robert Carter Nicholas, and George Wythe were only the most prominent of a "constellation of eminent lawyers and scholars" who practiced before the General Court in Williamsburg and were celebrated for their effectiveness as legislators. Other, only slightly less visible lawyers included John Blair, Jr., Dudley Digges, Joseph Jones, Henry Lee, and Thomson Mason.

There were fewer planters in this generation of leaders than in the previous one. But their number included the brilliant, ambitious, and hot-tempered orator Richard Henry Lee, three prominent James River planters, Benjamin Harrison V, Archibald Cary, and William Randolph, Jr., and two Potomac River residents who would gain national distinction during the Revolution, George Washington and George Mason. Like Robinson's generation, almost all of these men entered the House at a young age, mostly between twenty-six and thirty-three, and had long political careers.

Although Peyton Randolph's generation dominated Virginia political life at the beginning of the Revolution, it should be differentiated from a still younger generation that entered politics after the Revolutionary controversy had begun. This group included Carter Braxton, James Mercer, Patrick Henry, Severn Eyre, Thomas Jefferson, Thomas Nelson (the younger), James Madison, Edmund Randolph, John Marshall, and James Monroe.

Peyton Randolph.

These men began their legislative careers at a significantly younger age than members of previous generations of leaders. Not a single one of them had reached thirty when he first took his seat. Except for Braxton, who was a planter, and Nelson, who was a merchant, they were all lawyers, a fact which illustrates the growing importance of legal training as a qualification for a political career in the colony.

As their many achievements both in Virginia and in national politics attest, these leaders were men of considerable talent. Of the many men elected to the House of Burgesses in the late colonial period, only a few—perhaps ten to fifteen percent—managed to achieve a position of leadership. Serving on few committees and rarely speaking on the floor of the House, most members never left the back benches, where throughout their careers they sat in relative obscurity.

Selected not by the political community at large but by a small group of peers on the basis of intimate daily evaluations, those who aspired to become and to remain leaders had to show their fellows that they had certain qualities that distinguished them from the more ordinary men around them.

The high incidence of old gentry family names among House leaders might suggest that family and "pedigree" were the most important advantages in the competition for leadership positions within the House. But, as the cases of Edmund Pendleton, Patrick Henry, and James Madison make clear, one did not have to come from an old family to rise in the Virginia political establishment. Although wealth, family, and status might be sufficient to get a man elected to the House from some counties, ability and distinction were required to gain the confidence of the other members of the House and a place of leadership in that body.

Especially important was the ability to define political issues clearly, to devise strategies for coping with those issues, and to persuade fellow legislators to support those strategies. The capacity to elicit such support required skill in speaking and debate. With no organized parties to serve as a basis for mobilizing opinion, leaders had to depend very heavily upon persuasiveness of argument and the positive force of character to gain support for their views within the House.

Virtually all Virginia political leaders were impressive speakers and debaters. A few, like Richard Henry Lee and Patrick Henry, were inspired orators. Other related qualities were also significant. These included personal integrity, independence of mind, great diligence, an aptitude for business, and impressive learning, especially in the law.

Political Divisions

Modern Americans are accustomed to thinking of politics in terms of political parties. But parties of the kind we know today were a development of the nineteenth century. Eighteenth-century Virginia had no organized parties, and such occasional divisions as occurred within the House tended to revolve around personal attachments or differences in regional perspectives. During Robinson's long tenure as speaker, several leaders, including Peyton Randolph, Edmund Pendleton, Benjamin Harrison V, and Archibald Cary, were closely attached to him through ties of kinship and friendship and could almost always be counted on to vote for measures he supported.

But Robinson never tried to use these close associates as the nucleus of a political party. Rather, both he and his successor as speaker, Peyton Randolph, seem to have distributed committee positions and other duties widely according to merit and effectiveness rather than on the basis of political attachment. Intent on utilizing the full range of talents in the House, both gave key assignments to old men and young, experienced politicians and first-term legislators, men from old established and from new families, and men of all political persuasions, including independents and those who sometimes opposed them.

Although they could usually be counted on to vote with the speaker, independents consisted of those who prided themselves on voting according to what seemed best for the general welfare rather than according to partisan or sectional interests. Richard Bland, Benjamin Waller, George Wythe, and Robert Carter Nicholas were some of the more prominent independents during the last decades of the colonial era.

Opponents included those who often spoke and voted against the speaker and were potential political rivals. Charles Carter of Cleve, the last person to contest Robinson for the speakership back in 1742 and, next to Robinson, probably the most influential member of the House prior to his death in 1764, Landon Carter, Richard Henry Lee, who launched his career in the House in 1758 with a vigorous attack on Robinson, and Patrick Henry fall into this loose category. Robinson's willingness to give even those who disagreed with him important duties meant that the leadership of the House was quite broadly representative of all segments of the Virginia gentry.

These distinctions among independents, supporters, and opponents of the speaker were neither very firm nor clear-cut, and they never resulted in the development of permanent factions. At no time prior to the American Revolution, in fact, was there any issue of sufficient force to create more than temporary political divisions within the Virginia political establishment, and the colony's leaders continued to take pride in the fact that, as Sir John Randolph told the House of Burgesses in August 1734, the colony had "none of the perturbations which we see every where else arising from the different Views and Designs of Factions and Parties."

Far more important differences can be observed between two contrasting styles of political behavior. During the late colonial and Revolutionary eras, most Virginia leaders exhibited one or the other of two quite distinctive styles. The more dramatic of them was a product of the long quarrel with Britain in the years just prior to the Revolution. Epitomized by young firebrands like Richard Henry Lee, Patrick Henry, and Thomas Jefferson, it stood for vigor and forceful activity and stressed the necessity for resolution and uncompromising vigilance in defense of the most cherished possessions of the basic institutions and beliefs of the society.

The predominant style of leadership was much more sober. Exemplified by a large majority of Virginia's political leaders, including such experienced men as Speaker John Robinson, Richard Bland, Charles Carter of Cleve, Peyton Randolph, Edmund Pendleton, George Washington, George Wythe,

43

Patrick Henry.

Richard Henry Lee.

and Robert Carter Nicholas, as well as several younger men like James Madison, John Marshall, and Edmund Randolph, this style emphasized quiet deliberation, moderation, compromise, and the maintenance of stability in public life.

Such an emphasis and the style of leadership through which it was expressed seem to have been especially appropriate for a society like that of eighteenth-century Virginia. With almost no disagreement over fundamental socioeconomic or political objectives, Virginians did not look upon government as an active agent of change. Rather, they saw it as an instrument that would do little more than provide maximum scope for individual enterprise by guaranteeing the liberty of its members to pursue their own private interests in an orderly context and by securing to them the fruits of their enterprise.

The Imperatives of Politics

While practitioners of the more active style gave the Virginia political system its energy, those who exhibited this more sober style gave it stability. The latter style predominated among Virginia's political leaders during the late colonial and Revolutionary eras because it was so compatible with the colony's basic political objectives and beliefs.

First carefully worked out during the 1730s and 1740s by leaders and associates of Robinson's generation, these beliefs comprised an explicit political ideology that was passed along from one generation of leaders to the next and seems to have been widely endorsed not just by the leadership but also by voters and back benchers in the legislature. Of the many components of that ideology, five seem to have been of special importance: unanimity, moderation, virtue, independence, and loyalty.

Unanimity demanded the resolution of disputes in the interests of securing the peace and harmony of the polity. Believing, as Edmund Randolph would later remark, that it was unwise "ever to push to extremity any theory which by practical relations may not be accommodated" and that perfection was unattainable by mortal men, Virginians emphasized the importance of pragmatic compromise. When they could not "get the very best," they were willing to settle for "the best we can get." This impulse toward unanimity and compromise, they were persuaded, had enabled them to avoid those "private Broils" and "Party-Rancour" that characterized politics almost every-where else in the English-speaking world.

Moderation was no less important than unanimity as a basic political belief. Virginians took special pride in the "spirit of mildness" that, they liked to think, pervaded social relations among the free inhabitants and animated the colony's political life. Virginia politics, contemporaries claimed, was uniformly "cool and deliberate" and had no room for "violence and insub-ordination," those enemies to the quiet and stability of both public and private life.

Unanimity and moderation were in turn closely linked to two additional components of Virginia's underlying political ideology: loyalty and virtue. "Every political sentiment, every fashion in Virginia," said one observer, "appeared to be imper-fect unless it bore a resemblance to some precedent in England," and this "almost idolatrous deference to the mother country," Virginians preferred to believe, was reciprocated by "a particu-lar regard and predilection for Virginia" on the part of Britain.

For Virginians, however, the most important element of their basic political ideology, the central defining quality of their political system, was virtue. As one foreign traveler reported, by the last half of the eighteenth century, free Virginians conceived of themselves as having "an inborn higher morality" that had infused itself into the political system. Composed of fallible men, that system might occasionally make mistakes. But its leaders prided themselves upon the fact that Virginia was al-most wholly free of the political corruption that had tainted and eventually destroyed so many other political systems and that as political leaders they always tried to consider the welfare of the whole community rather than the particular interests of any of its parts.

The virtue of the political system also depended upon a fifth belief of fundamental importance: the much celebrated independence of Virginia's leaders. By the late colonial period, Edmund Randolph wrote, "a high sense of personal indepen-dence was universal" among white Virginians. Nourished by the "system of slavery, however so baneful to virtue," a "quick and acute sense" of personal liberty, a disdain for every "abridgement of personal independence," was, he thought, the "ornament" of the "real Virginia planter" and a distinguishing feature of the political character of Virginia.

As Randolph observed in a history of Virginia he wrote immediately after the Revolution, by the late colonial period

Virginia had long assumed such a pronounced air of "superiority over the [other] provinces" that the "pride of Virginia . . . had almost grown into a proverb." There were many sources of this pride. The first British colony to be settled in America and the first to be given royal status, it also had the most territory and people and was one of the wealthiest.

But there was no more important basis for Virginia's proud self-image than its achievements in the political realm. With so many experienced and talented leaders who had so successfully pursued and epitomized the values of unanimity, moderation, loyalty, virtue, and independence, Virginia "in a political view" was obviously "inferior to no other colony."

Crisis and Response, 1750–1776

Virginia's proud conception of itself was first shaken and then sharpened and reinforced by events and developments during the twenty-five years prior to the American Revolution. For all its achievements in the political realm, the social and economic position and self-image of the Virginia gentry were being increasingly threatened during this period by the behavior of its own members.

Especially disturbing was a perceptible falling away from the old values of industry, thrift, and sobriety and an exorbitant increase in luxury, gambling, and drunkenness. More and more through the middle decades of the eighteenth century, political leaders and clergymen remarked upon the growing "extravagance, ostentation, and . . . disregard for economy" among wealthier Virginians, some of whom were accumulating enormous debts to British merchants to pay for their lifestyles. No less frightening, drunkenness was rampant, and an uncontrollable "Passion . . . for Gaming . . . Racing, Cards, Dice and all other such Diversions" seemed to have broken out among people at all levels of society.

Especially evident among the rising generation, this widespread moral decline gave rise to a broadly diffused anxiety among the gentry about its moral claim to govern. Already by the early 1760s at the local level, so many justices of the peace were absenting themselves from the regular sessions of the county courts that it was difficult for the courts to meet to transact business.

Hunting was a favorite pastime of the Virginia gentry.
Courtesy, National Gallery of Art.

This obvious sacrifice of the public interest to private inclinations was particularly alarming because it occurred at the very time that a rapidly growing population and an increasing number of suits for debt were putting so much pressure on the courts that the number of days they had to be in session doubled or even tripled.

Although all of these developments ran directly counter to Virginia's image of itself as a society devoted to moderation, virtue, and independence, there were not yet in the early 1760s any obvious signs that they had seriously damaged the Virginia political system, at least not at the provincial level.

To be sure, several gentleman planters from old families—among them, William Byrd III and Benjamin Grymes—had already lost most of their estates and were bringing "ruin upon themselves [and their families] by their extravagance," gambling, and drinking. But the provincial government still appeared to be dominated by sober and upright men, many of whom had been performing capably and responsibly in positions of power for at least a generation.

At the same time that Virginia political leaders were becoming increasingly anxious about the internal moral state of Virginia society, various actions by the British government called into serious question the confident assumption that Britain "had a particular regard and predilection" for Virginia. Between 1759 and 1764, Virginians found themselves involved in two separate controversies.

The first was with British merchants over whether paper money issued by the colony in the late 1750s to pay for its heavy contribution to the Seven Years' War between 1754 and 1763 should be legal tender in payment of debts to British creditors. The second was with a minority of the Virginia clergy over the legislature's right to pay clerical salaries in money rather than in tobacco, the legal medium of payment.

British officials had power to veto any laws passed in Virginia, and in both of these controversies they sided with the colony's opponents and thereby acted to undermine the author-

Patrick Henry argued the "Parson's Cause" in the Hanover County courthouse.
Courtesy, Virginia Historical Society.

48

ity of the Virginia legislature over the internal affairs of the colony. As lieutenant governor, Fauquier aligned himself with the Virginia political establishment in both of these conflicts, and his behavior helped to prevent significant erosion of Virginia loyalty to Britain.

But these events created heightened resentment of British interference in Virginia affairs and mounting suspicions of British intentions toward the colony. They thereby ate away at the foundations of Virginia's celebrated British patriotism.

Certainly they also contributed in 1764–1766 to Virginia's strong response to the Stamp Act, Britain's first attempt to tax the colonies for revenue. Along with leaders of other colonies, Virginians quickly saw that, contrary to their rights as free British subjects, this measure subjected them to taxation by the British Parliament, a body in which they were not represented.

By so doing, moreover, it also undermined the hitherto exclusive right of colonial legislatures to tax the inhabitants of the colonies. With customary moderation, the Virginia legislature in December 1764 sent firm protests to the king and both branches of Parliament and thereby joined the New York Assembly as the first American legislature to protest the constitutionality of the Stamp Act.

When these and similar petitions from other colonies failed to deter Parliament from passing the Stamp Act, the House of Burgesses in May 1765 adopted a series of bold resolutions denouncing the act as illegal and destructive of the most basic rights of Virginians as Britons. Introduced by Patrick Henry during his very first session in the House, these resolutions passed over the opposition of Speaker Robinson and other senior House leaders who objected to their immoderate tone.

More than any action taken by any other American legislature, however, Henry's resolutions provided a rallying call for uncompromising resistance to the Stamp Act. Serving as a model for similar resolutions from most of the other colonies, they placed Virginia at the forefront of the opposition of the thirteen American colonies that led to repeal of the measure in early 1766.

Virginia's active and unswerving opposition to the Stamp Act helped enormously to reaffirm its ancient self-image. It seemed to make clear that, to whatever extent Virginia society was weakened by luxury and pleasure, the colony's political system still had sufficient vigor—and virtue—to dare to stand up to oppression.

This British satire pokes fun at the Stamp Act.

That Virginians, far from having yet become so "unmanly . . . as to yield to such impositions," had in fact taken the lead in opposing them was greatly satisfying to the colony's political leaders. Over the next twenty-five years, that satisfaction encouraged Virginians to continue to try to take leading roles in the critical events of the Revolutionary era.

Within a few weeks after the repeal of the Stamp Act, however, Virginia's political leaders were confronted with new doubts about the legitimacy of their claims both to public virtue and to the confidence of the society they governed. In May 1766, the death of Speaker Robinson led to the discovery that he had loaned to his friends over £100,000 from public funds entrusted to him as treasurer, perhaps the most flagrant example of political corruption in the entire history of the British-American colonies prior to the Revolution.

The disclosure of corruption of such magnitude might have divided the Virginia political establishment into embittered factions or even destroyed it politically, and some feared that that was precisely what would happen.

But the establishment's reaction was both vigorous and self-critical. A reformist group within it led a successful campaign to get to the bottom of the Robinson scandal and to prevent similar occurrences in the future by detaching the treasury from the speakership. Through their strong exertions, these men managed in 1766 to reestablish, more firmly than ever perhaps, the credibility of the establishment's long-standing claims to political dominance. By so doing, it insured that Virginia political leadership would continue to be sufficiently united to spearhead the opposition to Britain over the next decade.

Nor was that unity shattered by new religious divisions that affected the colony beginning in the mid-1760s. Increasingly thereafter, militant Baptists began to make significant inroads in the Virginia countryside. By their simple lifestyles, their forceful denunciation of the existing Anglican religious establishment, and their enthusiastic religious preaching, they directly challenged existing social mores in fundamental ways.

Moreover, by their powerful demands for full toleration and separation of church and state, they thrust religion into the political arena, where it remained an issue of substance until they achieved their objectives almost two decades later. But the Baptist challenge did not alter existing patterns of political activity in Virginia and, in fact, helped to reinforce the traditional emphasis upon compromise as a device for achieving unanimity.

So secure was Virginia's political leadership during these years that when the Revolution finally came in 1776, it produced not a rejection but an overwhelming endorsement of that leadership. Reinvigorated by its handling of the Stamp Act crisis and the Robinson scandal in 1765–1766, that leadership was able, in the midst of a revolutionary upheaval, to infuse traditional political modes and ideals into a new state government and to carry out still further reforms in Virginia's social and political system without either altering in any fundamental way the existing structure of politics or losing the confidence of Virginia society.

On the national level, no state, not even Massachusetts, contributed so heavily and so conspicuously to the leadership of the Revolution and to the organization of the new nation. The prominence of Virginians in national political councils for a half-century beginning with the first tentative establishment of an American nation in the mid-1770s stands as the strongest possible testimony to the vitality and effectiveness of the eighteenth-century Virginia political system.

Further Reading

Raymond C. Bailey, *Popular Influence upon Public Policy: Petitioning in Eighteenth-Century Virginia* (Westport, Conn., 1979).

Carl Bridenbaugh, *Myths and Realities: Societies of the Colonial South* (Baton Rouge, La., 1952).

Robert E. and B. Katherine Brown, *Virginia 1705–1786: Democracy or Aristocracy?* (East Lansing, Mich., 1964).

Jack P. Greene, "Character, Persona, and Authority: A Study of Alternative Styles of Political Leadership in Revolutionary Virginia," in W. Robert Higgins, ed., *The Revolutionary War in the South: Power, Conflict, and Leadership: Essays in Honor of John Richard Alden* (Durham, N. C., 1979).

———, "Foundations of Political Power in the Virginia House of Burgesses, 1720–1776," *William and Mary Quarterly*, 3rd Ser., XVI (October 1959), pp. 485–506.

———, *Landon Carter, An Inquiry into the Personal Values and Social Imperatives of the Eighteenth-Century Virginia Gentry* (Charlottesville, Va., 1965).

———, *The Quest for Power: The Lower Houses of Assembly in the Southern Royal Colonies, 1689–1776* (Chapel Hill, N.C., 1963).

———, "Society, Ideology, and Politics: An Analysis of Political Culture of Mid-Eighteenth-Century Virginia," in Richard M. Jellison, ed., *Society, Freedom, and Conscience: The American Revolution in Virginia, Massachusetts, and New York* (New York, 1976), pp. 14–76, 190–201.

———, " 'Veritus et Libertas': Political Culture, Social Change, and the Origins of the American Revolution in Virginia, 1763–1776," in Jeffrey J. Crow and Larry E. Tise, eds., *The Southern Experience in the American Revolution* (Chapel Hill, N. C., 1978), pp. 55–108.

Lucille Griffith, *The Virginia House of Burgesses 1750–1774*, (University, Ala., 1968).

Rhys Isaac, *The Transformation of Virginia 1740–1790* (Chapel Hill, N. C., 1982).

Edmund S. Morgan, *American Slavery, American Freedom: The Ordeal of Colonial Virginia* (New York, 1975).

A. G. Roeber, *Faithful Magistrates and Republican Lawyers: Creators of Virginia Legal Culture, 1680–1810* (Chapel Hill, N. C., 1981).

Herbert Sloan and Peter Onuf, "Politics, Culture, and the Revolution in Virginia: A Review of Recent Work," *Virginia Magazine of History and Biography*, XIC (July 1983), pp. 259–284.

Daniel Blake Smith, *Inside the Great House: Planter Family Life in Eighteenth-Century Chesapeake Society* (Ithaca, N. Y., 1980).

Charles S. Sydnor, *Gentlemen Freeholders: Political Life in Washington's Virginia* (Chapel Hill, N. C., 1952).

Thad W. Tate, "The Coming of the Revolution in Virginia: Britain's Challenge to Virginia's Ruling Class, 1763–1776," *William and Mary Quarterly*, 3rd Ser., XIX (July 1962), pp. 323–343.

Thad W. Tate and David L. Ammerman, eds., *The Chesapeake in the Seventeenth Century: Essays on Anglo-American Society* (Chapel Hill, N. C., 1979).

Louis B. Wright, *The First Gentlemen of Virginia: Intellectual Qualities of the Early Colonial Ruling Class* (San Marino, Calif., 1940).